Ike
Takes Flight

Karl J. Kuerner

Wilmington, Delaware

Ike
Takes Flight

First Printing

Published by:
Cedar Tree Books, Ltd.
Wilmington, Delaware 19807
books@ctpress.com
www.cedartreebooks.com

ISBN 978-1-892142-53-5

Title: Ike Takes Flight
Author: Karl J. Kuerner
Editor: Nick Cerchio
Book Design: Bob Schwartz

Copyright © 2012 Cedar Tree Books

Printed and bound in the United States of America

All rights reserved. No part of this book may be used, reproduced or transmitted in any form without written permission of the author and the publisher, except in the case of brief quotations embodied in critical essays and reviews.

Dedication

Again to those who have been so special in helping create a second book about a little cat named Ike.

Ike has made himself a fixture in the Kuerner home greeting guests and friends alike (except at night). His antics are becoming quite well known. So to Ike himself, "thanks."

To Jim Koonz who spent eons taking Ike's picture.

To all friends, feline and human alike, much appreciation.

Karl J. Kuerner
2012

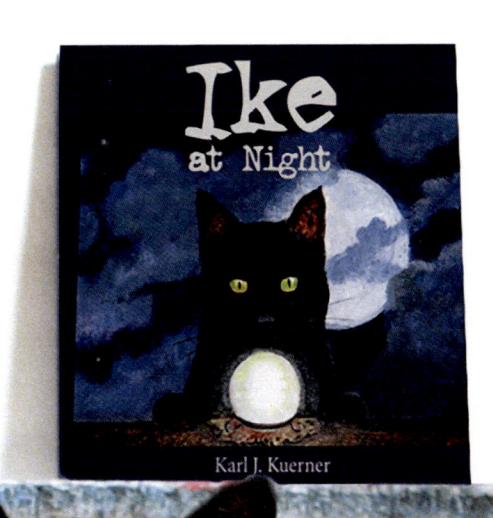

Oh little black cat off you go. Only this time it is into the air, wouldn't you know?

How you got this crazy little dream is way beyond me.

And then again, maybe it's a scheme to see what you can see!!

KJK
2012

Ike
Takes Flight

Is this a dream...

or just a deep sleep?

But something has caught Ike's attention.

And he thinks

    it's real neat.

Just what will

Ike do in his dream?

Will he let it

take him away?

Of

course!!!

That's what

dreams do!!!

And

suddenly

he's

gone.

And up he goes.

For dreams can take you anywhere

                  over hill and dale

                                    and valleys below.

Even the flowers wave a friendly hello!!!

Flying with birds

is neat too.

He sees

his buddies

below.

So why

   not

      pick

         them

            up

For

the

ride

of

their

lives?

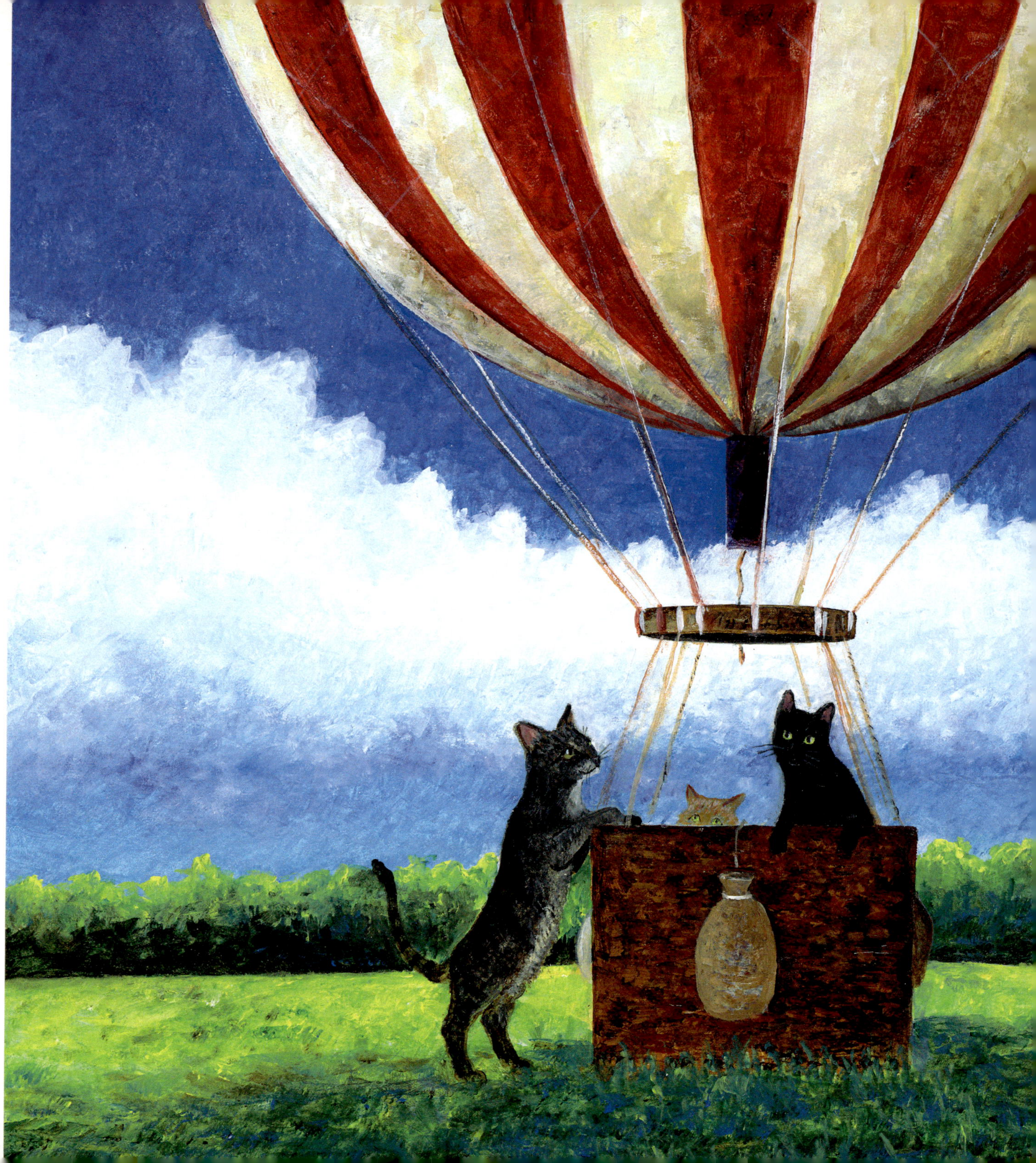

For it's great

to share dreams.

Ike's flight

takes them

above the

storm

and through

the rain.

They're all safe...

For it's only a

dream...

Or is it!!!???

Uh

Oh

Fog!!!

Where to now?

The world awaits

Ike's dream.

And over the rainbow they go

where

anything

is possible.

You can turn the

world

upside

down!!!

Flying through

fireworks

For

dreams

are

good

day

or

night

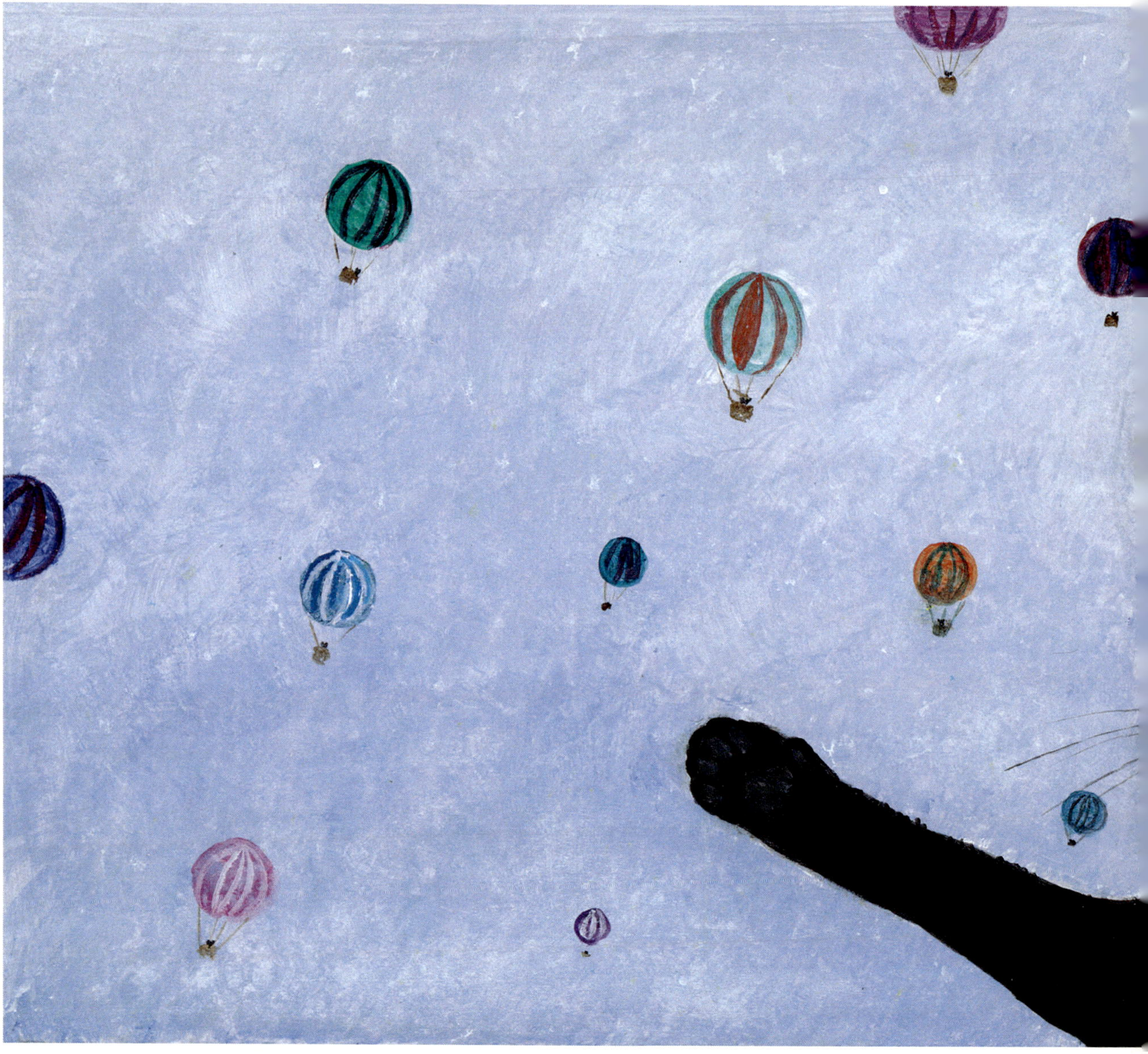

Goggles anyone?

Was this really a dream or a deep sleep?

Well...

　　Another

　　　　day

Now what?

Colophon

Ike Takes Flight was designed in Italy by Bob Schwartz on an Apple MacPro using Adobe InDesign and Photoshop CS5. The text was set in 18 point Ghostwriter twenty-two point leaded.

This edition was digitally printed and bound in the United States of America by TFR Printing of Dayton, Ohio on 100# gloss text.